MUSLI...

992972952 6

This edition 2003

Franklin Watts
96 Leonard Street
London
EC2A 4XD

Franklin Watts Australia
45-51 Huntley Street
Alexandria
NSW 2015

Copyright © 1988 Franklin Watts

Design: Edward Kinsey
Typesetting: Tradespools Ltd

All rights reserved. No part of this publication may be reproduced, stored in a retrieval system, or transmitted in any form or by any means, electronic, mechanical, photocopy, recording or otherwise, without the prior written permission of the copyright owner.

A CIP catalogue record for this book is available from the British Library.

ISBN: 0 7496 5044 3

Printed in Italy

The publisher would like to thank the Nazir family and all other people shown in this book.

Note: Many of the photographs in this book originally appeared in 'My Belief: I am a Muslim'

Our Culture

Muslim

Jenny Wood

Photographs: Chris Fairclough
Consultant: Sheikh Jamal M.A. Solaiman

FRANKLIN WATTS
LONDON•SYDNEY

GLOUCESTERSHIRE COUNTY LIBRARY	
9929729526	
PETERS	07-Feb-06
297	£5.99

These people are Muslims.
They follow a religion called Islam
which began in Arabia
over a thousand years ago.

Islam was begun
by the prophet Muhammad
who lived in the Arab city of Mecca.
Mecca is now the holy city of Islam.

Muslims believe that God's message,
as spoken to Muhammad,
is written in the Koran,
their Holy Book.
The Muslim name for God is Allah.

Muslims must wear clothes that cover their bodies.
A man must cover his body from the waist to the knees.

A Muslim woman must cover herself
from head to toe,
except for her hands and face.
Many Muslim women wear a long tunic
over loose trousers.

This is a mosque.
Muslims come here to worship Allah.
Mosques usually have a dome
and a tower called a minaret.

Before entering the mosque, Muslims must take off their shoes.

Muslims have to make sure they are clean before praying to Allah. They wash their hands, face, arms, head, ears, and finally their feet.

When they pray, Muslims
must face Mecca, their holy city.
They sit on special prayer mats.
The prayers are led by an Imam.

Prayers last for about ten minutes. Women are not allowed to pray with the men. They worship in a different part of the mosque.

Every mosque has a Koran school, where Muslim children learn to read their Holy Book. Muslims must live according to the rules of the Koran.

The Koran is written in Arabic script. The pages are often beautifully decorated.

Muslims read the Koran at home too. They keep their copies of the Koran wrapped in cloth, so that they do not get dirty.

Muslims must pray to Allah five times a day. At home, as in the mosque, Muslims take off their shoes and wash themselves.

Muslims have to obey special rules about food. They are not allowed to eat pork. All other meat must be prepared in a special way, known as "Halal".

Favourite meals are curries, kebabs and rice.

All Muslims wash and say prayers before and after a meal.
The eldest person in the family starts eating first.

A Muslim wedding is very colourful.
The bride dresses in red.
After the ceremony,
there is a wedding feast.

The bridegroom wears a special head-dress. He gives a gift of money to his bride.

Muslims like to study the many books on the teachings of Muhammad and the rules of Islam.
They try to follow all the rules and become good Muslims.

FACTS ABOUT MUSLIMS

Islam, the Muslim religion, is the second largest religion in the world. It has about 600 million followers.

In Britain, there are about one million Muslims. They come mainly from Pakistan, Bangladesh, India, and West and East Africa.

Muslims believe that the Koran contains the word of Allah, as told to the prophet Muhammad. Muhammad lived in the holy city of Mecca over a thousand years ago.

There are five things which all Muslims must do during their lifetime.
1. They must say that they believe there is no God but Allah.
2. They must say their prayers five times a day.
3. They must give money to the poor.
4. They must go without food or drink between dawn and dusk during the month of Ramadan, the ninth month in the Muslim year.
5. They must visit the holy city of Mecca.

GLOSSARY

Allah
The Muslim name for God.

Arabic
The language of the Arabs. The Koran is written in Arabic.

Halal
An Arabic word, meaning "allowed". It is used to describe food that has been prepared according to Muslim laws.

Imam
The person who leads the prayers in the mosque.

Islam
The Muslim religion.

Koran
The Muslim Holy Book.

Mecca
The Muslim holy city. It is in Saudi Arabia.

Mosque
The Muslim place of worship.

Muhammad
The founder of the religion of Islam.

Prophet
A religious teacher.

INDEX

Alcohol 27
Allah 9, 12, 14, 20, 27, 28
Arabic 18, 28

Clothes 10

Food 21, 27, 28

God 9, 27, 28

Halal 21, 28
Holy Book 9, 17, 28

Imam 15, 28
Islam 7, 8, 26, 27, 28

Koran 9, 17, 18, 19, 27, 28
Koran school 17

Mecca 8, 15, 27, 28
Minaret 12
Mosque 12, 13, 16, 17, 20, 28
Muhammad 8, 9, 26, 27, 28

Prayer 15, 16, 23, 27, 28
Prayer mat 15
Prophet 8, 27, 28

Ramadan 27

Saudi Arabia 28

Wash 14, 20, 23
Wedding 24
Women 11, 16